Woman to Woman

IF YOU OWN IT, CLAIM IT!
SUCCESS!

*A Beginner's Inspirational Guide
for Women Seeking to
Start Their Own
Business*

JANIE C. JESSEE

JCP

Jan-Carol
Publishing, Inc

"every story needs a book"

Woman to Woman
Janie C. Jessee

Published April 2019
Express Editions
All rights reserved
Cover Design by Tara Sizemore
Copyright © 2019 by Janie C. Jessee

ISBN: 978-1-945619-99-1

You may contact the publisher:
Jan-Carol Publishing, Inc.
PO Box 701
Johnson City, TN 37605
publisher@jancarolpublishing.com
jancarolpublishing.com

*This is dedicated to all women
with an entrepreneurial spirit!*

Always be your Best Friend

Words to guide you each day: You are what you tell yourself. Look in the mirror, and the person you see looking back at you can be your best friend or your worst enemy. Choose her to be your best friend. Start on a journal of your accomplishments and your talents. This will reinforce goals and your hopes and dreams.

> *"There are plenty of difficult obstacles in your path—don't allow yourself to become one of them."*
> Ralph Marston, American Writer

> *"What you tell yourself, you will believe."*
> Unknown

Believe in Yourself

What is in your heart? What are your hobbies? Do you have a vision? Does it help others? What's your motivation? Ask these questions to the person you see in mirror. That person looking back at you in the mirror knows you better than ANYONE. She knows you because she knows your heart.

"A girl should be two things:
who and what she wants."

Coco Chanel, *The Gospel According to Coco Chanel:*
Life Lessons from the World's Most Elegant Woman

"I am beautiful; I am smart;
I can do ANYTHING that is in my heart!"

Janie C. Jessee, author, business owner

Confidence comes from Within

What is your confidence rooted in? Does someone tell you that you are not smart? That you are ugly? Has someone discouraged you and told you that you can't or won't amount to anything? Start a journal of your accomplishments and your talents. See yourself as the special person you are!

"If you don't own it, don't claim it.
If you own it, claim it!"

Janie C. Jessee, author, business owner

"I will define my own success!"

Janie C. Jessee, author, business owner

Decide for Yourself

Surround yourself with positive people and those who will encourage you, but the decision to start your own business has to be your decision. Write down the pros and cons for starting your business. This will set a pathway for you to branch out and grow in your talents. Listening to others' advice doesn't mean that you have to live by it. Just listen, and then decide for yourself.

"Give yourself permission to be successful!"
Janie C. Jessee, author, business owner

"Today is my day in my success."
Janie C. Jessee, author, business owner

Enthusiasm is Contagious

Y ou can't expect everyone to share in your enthusiasm for starting your own business, so become your own biggest cheerleader. If you are not proud of what you are doing, how can you expect others to share your joy? You are a pioneer, and you are exploring an unknown territory! This is exciting!

"I like me this way!"

Janie C. Jessee, author, business owner

"Love yourself first and everything else falls into line. You really have to love yourself to get anything done in this world."

Lucille Ball

Fear isn't a Stop Sign

Fear is a real emotion. It can be debilitating, crippling, and immobilizing, and it has roots. Are you feeding your fear? Where does your fear originate? Just as trees have roots that require water, sun, and nutrients to grow, your fear has roots and requires to be fed. Feed your fear with empowering words, and you will branch out with confidence. By knowing the root of the fear, you can turn that Fear into Fearless.

"Root yourself in this motto:
F*-feel* **E***-encouraged* **A***-always—* **R***-repeat = FEAR*
*Feel Encouraged Always—**repeat**!"*
Janie C. Jessee, author, business owner

"Obstacles are not stop signs, just detours."
Janie C. Jessee, author, business owner

Go For it—Set your GPS

To be successful, you must set your GPS— GOT to PLAN for SUCCESS! Just as you use a GPS to get to a destination, starting a new career or a new business requires preparation, planning, and an outline of what you are hoping to accomplish and how to arrive at your destination—Success! Plan for the unexpected twists and turns along your way.

> *"If you do not know where you are going, how will you know when you get there?"*
> Unknown

> *"You have to crawl before you walk and walk before you run!"*
> Unknown

Heart to Heart

Disappointments will happen. Surprises will cause you heartaches. But just as flowers need the sunny days, flowers need the rain to wash away the dirt and dust and grow stronger and brighter. Give yourself permission to cry, feel the pain, and recognize the hurt. But you do not give the disappointments permission to control you or stop you.

"The way I see it, if you want the rainbow, you gotta put up with the rain."

Dolly Parton, country singer, actress, businesswoman

"When you have a dream you've got to grab it and never let go."

Carol Burnett, actress

Image

How do you see yourself? Doctors and nurses are expected to dress for their profession. Bankers and lawyers have a universal dress code. Rock stars shine in their style of dress. Like it or not, people form opinions and judgments on appearance. So, while you should keep your personality in your style, dress the part. How do others see you? Image is part of your success. Can't afford to dress like a million dollars? Buy the best for less at thrift stores, consignment shops, and close outs.

"I dress in the best for less, and myself I always impress."

Janie C. Jessee, author, business owner

"You can have anything you want in life, if you dress for it."

Edith Head, American costume designer

Jealousy

Be on the lookout for jealousy. The truth is that friends may become enemies and enemies may become friends because of their rejection or acceptance of your goals and successes. Jealousy is a strong emotional weapon that women put to action against other women. Once jealousy is in your heart, it is hard to remain focused on what you can do and grow your goals. It cheats you, deceives you, and steals your joy. You do have a choice. Don't become a part of a tangled web of jealousy. Take the high road in your high heels, and step over those with jealousy because it doesn't fit in your pathway.

"Jealousy is the ice on a slick road; steer clear of it."

Janie C. Jessee, author, business owner

"The person who said that the truth never hurts never knew the truth."

Janie C. Jessee, author, business owner

Know your Strengths and your Weaknesses

Keep your eyes on your goals. You can achieve your goals by turning weaknesses into strengths, if you recognize them. Acknowledge what you can do, and accept the things that are not as easy for you to do. What are your hobbies? What are you passionate about? These strengths can quickly push those weaknesses aside. Your strengths define you— what you can do rather than what you feel that you cannot do.

> *"Look at what you can do—*
> *not what you cannot."*
>
> Unknown

> *"Step up with your strengths, and they will overshadow any weakness, and then allow weaknesses to become strengths."*
>
> Janie C. Jessee, author, business owner

Let it go!

What baggage are you carrying around with you? What is in your way of reaching for your dreams? Is there something in your past that has convinced you that you cannot move forward? Let it go. Put it where it needs to be—buried in the past. Yesterday is gone, and tomorrow begins with what you do today.

"You can't look forward while looking back."
Unknown

"The truth is, unless you let go, unless you forgive yourself, unless you forgive the situation, unless you realize that the situation is over, you cannot move forward."
Steve Maraboli, *Unapologetically You: Reflections on Life and the Human Experience*

Moral Compass

If your hopes, dreams, and mission are in alignment with your moral compass, then reaching your success will be a journey worth traveling. Do you have an anchor point in your life and a code of ethics that you live by? You must stand strong on your morals and principles because they will be tested and twisted by those without a conscious. Do not be destroyed by the unworthy.

"Do not be deceived: bad company corrupts good morals."

Anonymous, Holy Bible: King James Version

"I create my platform of principles, my foundation of morals, and my core of values that will not be in agreement with all, but is in agreement with my soul."

Janie C. Jessee, author, business owner

Negativity

Yes—we all can be negative at times. Do you see the glass half empty rather than half full? A lifestyle of living to see the positive must be formed as a habit. This means that you can change your attitude. Habits are broken, created, and changed. When a negative thought crosses your mind, get in the habit of asking yourself how you can change it into a positive thought. You may be surprised how quickly the positive attitude lessens the negative attitude.

"On this day, do you seek the sunshine or drown in the possibility of rain? Your choice."

Janie C. Jessee, author, business owner

"All days are good. It is just some good days are better than the other good days."

Unknown

Optimism

Optimism is rooted in happiness. Is someone or something stealing your joy? Starting each day with an uplifting song, bible verse, or quote will create the temperature of your day. When the overload is almost too much to carry, finding humor will lighten your load.

"Don't cry because it's over, smile because it happened."

Dr. Seuss

"You laugh and you cry, but either way, you are responsible for your own happiness!"

Janie C. Jessee, author, business owner

Plan with Purpose and Promise

You must plan for success. The purpose of your planning is your foundation to your success. Do you promise to do your best? Outlining your course, following your vision, and making a promise to yourself that you will reach your destination will strengthen your determination to succeed. Plan your goals with a purpose of fulfilling your promises and promise to do your best.

> *"Promises should not be broken, especially the promises you make to yourself."*
>
> Janie C. Jessee, author, business owner

> *"We all have a purpose in life, and when you find yours you will recognize it."*
>
> Unknown

Question to Seek Answers

If you ask questions, you will hear and learn things. It is the right answer to the right question that determines how you can move forward in business. Knowledge is power, and asking questions will give you information. Instead of answering questions, become a person who can ask questions. This is very useful in making conservation and, at the same time, gathering knowledge. Speak up, and do not fear the answer when you ask a question. Learning and gaining knowledge will unlock doors that are locked. You ask; others will share.

"Ask, and it shall be given to you; seek, and ye shall find; knock, and it shall be opened unto you: For every one that asketh receiveth; and he that seeketh findeth; and to him that knocketh it shall be opened."
King James Bible, Matthew 7:8

"Ask yourself the questions, and answer yourself with the answers that are positive and encouraging to you."
Janie C. Jessee, author, business owner

Root yourself in Resiliency

Life is like a chalk board. Living life is the chalk writing 'stuff' on the chalk board. The chalk board gets so full, there's no space to write anything more. You're overwhelmed. Give yourself permission to 'cry the tears' and wash the board clean and clear. It is then that you refresh, redirect, and move forward. Resiliency is being able to rest, bouncing back, and never quitting.

"The oak fought the wind and was broken, the willow bent when it must and survived."

Robert Jordan, *The Fires of Heaven*

"Just as a branch on a tree may break, the trunk of the tree sways through the storm and endures because of its roots."

Janie C. Jessee, author, business owner

Success

How do you define success? Success means different things to different people. There's no room for comparison. In comparison, there will always be better and worse. You cannot be trapped by another's definition. You own your success by your terms and not another's imposed definition of success. Success is in the eyes of the beholder.

"Don't stand in your own way of success by not recognizing it."

Janie C. Jessee, author, business owner

"Success is largely a matter of holding on after others have let go."

Unknown

Time

Time is priceless, yet it is the most valuable asset you will have. Take time, give time, and make time. Timing is everything in everything you do and create. Do not wait on time, do not waste your time, and set time to go after your dreams and goals.

"Yesterday's disappointments will steal today if you allow it to become your tomorrow."

Janie C. Jessee, author, business owner

"Time is free, but it's priceless. You can't own it, but you can use it."

Unknown

Uncertainty

Uncertainty is like an unpromising. We are not promised a tomorrow, and we are not certain that we have today. Nothing is certain except taxes and death. We take risks every day. Taking a step toward your dreams and goals will be a step into the unknown. The remedy to replacing doubt and apprehension is to take a risk. Be confident in taking a risk, and the uncertainty will disappear in the shadows.

"Taking a risk is like taking your first roller coaster ride. Will it end, and will you do it again? But when the ride stops, the risk was worth it."

Janie C. Jessee, author, business owner

"Sometimes the wrong choices bring us to the right places."

Unknown

Vision

How do you see yourself? That vision of yourself is your portrait in business and as a person. Align your vision of yourself to the person you want to be, the accomplishments you seek, and the picture of success you wish to attain. If you see yourself as successful, then you are.

"I see it, therefore it is."

Janie C. Jessee, author, business owner

"Have a vision. It is the ability to see the invisible. If you can see the invisible, you can achieve the impossible."

Shiv Khera

Worry

Worry is a thief. It steals your creativity, your time, your energy, and most of all, your will. If you worry about the 'what if's' with a negative attitude, turn the 'what if's' into a positive attitude. You should not ask 'what if I fail,' but rather 'what if I succeed?' This replaces worry with joy and enthusiasm.

"Stop worrying about what can go wrong, and get excited about what can go right."

Unknown

*"Worry stands for **W**ill **O**vercome **R**ationally, **R**elentlessly **Y**earlong!"*

Janie C. Jessee, author, business owner

Xenodochial–means Friendly to Strangers

Seek to learn something new every day and meet a new person every day. The more people you meet, the larger your network becomes. Take an interest in others, and others will remember you. You can learn something from everyone you meet. All will not become friends, and some may become enemies, but building a foundation in friendliness will open the doors you thought to be closed.

"They may forget what you said–but they will never forget how you made them feel."

Carl W. Buehner

"The smile you give a stranger today may be the encouragement they need for the rest of their life."

Janie C. Jessee, author, business owner

Yielding

D o not yield into the temptation of giving up or accepting defeat. When a storm hits your pathway, you bend, but you do not break. Yield to strength, solitude, and action. Action yields results. From the worst experiences to the smallest victories, the gains yielded from each will transform your discouragement to encouragement.

"The pain you feel today is the strength you feel tomorrow."

Unknown

"I yield to my faith, my hope, and my convictions, and then I yield to the rewards."

Janie C. Jessee, author, business owner

ZigZag

The journey to success is not a straight and narrow pathway. The journey will have twists and turns, hills and valleys, and dark and light curves. The journey will have calmness and conflicts, fairness and unfairness, and also, welcomed happiness and joys. How you combine the zigs and zags can ultimately develop a superior performance for keeping you on track.

"Do what you can, with what you have, where you are."

Theodore Roosevelt

"The brightly zigzagged threads sown in my daily life are the ropes that I hold onto for my tomorrows."

Janie C. Jessee, author, business owner

I Believe...

*"But thou shalt remember the LORD thy God:
for it is he that giveth thee power to get wealth,
which he may establish his covenant which
he swore unto thy fathers, as it is this day."*

Deuteronomy 8:18, King James Version

*"And Jesus said unto them...
'If ye have faith as a grain of mustard seed,
ye shall say unto this mountain,
Remove hence to yonder place; and
it shall remove; and nothing shall be
impossible to you.'"*

Romans 1:17, King James Version

❧

www.ingramcontent.com/pod-product-compliance
Lightning Source LLC
Chambersburg PA
CBHW021917190326
41519CB00008B/810